CONTENTS

Tea, Fags, and Poetry

Tea, Fags, and Poetry

AL DRAPER

authorHOUSE®

AuthorHouse™ UK
1663 Liberty Drive
Bloomington, IN 47403 USA
www.authorhouse.co.uk
Phone: 0800.197.4150

Published by AuthorHouse 12/18/2014

ISBN: 978-1-4969-9941-2 (sc)
ISBN: 978-1-4969-9940-5 (hc)
ISBN: 978-1-4969-9942-9 (e)

My Children Gemma, Anthony, Lily & George. My Sister Janet and my friend Tracie for listening to me.

.

INTRODUCTION

Many would describe my childhood as dysfunctional. I call it colourful. My adult life was to be more colourful than I could have ever imagined. At the age of 15, I became pregnant with my first child. I was just a baby myself. This was when I was told my life was over, but luckily, I didn't agree. Life was never easy for me, but I always felt blessed. I knew I would be okay, even when faced with tragedy and life events which at times seemed unbelievable.

Having grown up around mental illness and also having lost a brother to suicide, I have always pondered my own behaviour. On occasion, I have battled with my own suicidal thoughts when life seemed unbearable, pulling myself back to some kind of normality for the sake of my children, through the power of my own thoughts and self-belief.

In 2010, I suffered from post-traumatic stress disorder (PTSD), which remained undiagnosed until 2014. I spent two years of my life battling with the nightmares of the traumatic events which led to this horrific emotional and debilitating condition. When I recovered, I felt compelled to help my fellow human beings with whatever sufferings they wished to expose, confront, and eradicate. Eventually, I trained to become a hypnotherapist.

My mum suffered with bipolar disorder. Until recently, depression carried a stigma, and the available help and understanding were limited. It broke my heart each and every time I watched her illness envelop her mind and body. She was 77 when she died on 24 March 2014.

When my mum died, I could not accept it; although vulnerable, she was the strongest woman I had ever met. She filled such a big part of my life that I had a hole in my heart the size of the Grand Canyon. I carried on with life, just as many people do after such a loss. I found it hard to cry, as that would confirm she was dead. I have to say that I did have her ashes in my living room, but that wasn't working for me. For me, she was still here; I just could not see her.

Barbara

They said you were gone, I did not believe;

Too painful the words for my mind to conceive.

I walked behind horses, followed by masses;

Now all I have left in my hand are your ashes.

I cannot accept it; I know it is fate,

so I write down these words to open the gate.

For the tears have to flow, and the wound has to heal;

I have to embrace just how I feel.

Rejoice in the joy that you're like no other,

Alive in my mind, my beautiful mother.

(Barbara Hilditch 1937–2014)

CHAPTER 1

The Call

Grief can take many forms. Like many people who lose a loved one, I could not accept it. I could hear her voice echoing through the silence: "Listen to your mum." In my mind's eye, I could see her laughing. I didn't even need to close my eyes. But, most of all, I could feel her – she was not gone. She was here; right next to my side, an invisible shadow no one could see. Only I could tell she was there.

Three weeks passed quickly after her death, and I still felt the same. "She is not gone," I would tell my sister. "I can feel her."

What happened next took me by surprise. I had barely opened my eyes to face the day one morning, when out of the blue, my thoughts began to rhyme. I ignored it at first, but everything I thought rhymed.

So I grabbed a pen and wrote it down. Three minutes later, another rhyme came. And another.

Three hours later, holding eleven poems in my hand, I rang my friend Tracie.

"Guess what?" Before she could answer, I gushed, "I'm a poet!"

"Cool," she said.

Neither of us knew it at the time, but I was about to write over seventy poems during a three-day period. I will never know where the words came from, but I was left feeling a peace inside that I had never experienced, along with a newfound love of poetry.

The Call

He gave me the pen,

saying, "Write on the wall."

I wrote down the staircase

and into the hall.

The fire inside me,

full blaze and alight.

My gut full of gravel,

smothering fright.

You ask, "Was it madness?"

I reply, "Not at all."

Don't be afraid,

it's

only

The Call.

Tea, fags, and poetry,

could life be much finer?

Chamomile tea

in delicate china,

quenching the thirst

of a word-hungry

rhymer.

Words become senses

alive on the page.

Visions of lovers

act out on a stage.

Will you connect?

What will you see?

Tea, fags, and poetry;

the time

I share

me.

When Rhyme Is a Crime

Entering the lion's den,

My only weapon is a pen.

Three days seem like a long, long time;

That's when I started writing rhyme.

I have to share this, things got bad;

My friends think I am going mad.

As they talk, my mind's elsewhere;

I seem to have a vacant stare.

My house is a tip, a volcanic eruption;

Shh! I said no interruption.

Poetry, it's all your doing;

If it does not end, I will be suing.

Lost

The vacant space where once you lay;

The silent void, no more to say.

The absence of the tender kiss;

The loving arms are what I'll miss.

The gentle breeze now fills the space;

The warming sun a new embrace.

In fact, this is one of the great secrets of our time.

The ties that bind beyond the sky.

Destiny

I didn't know I was travelling. …

When I got off the train,

The journey was done;

I never laid the blame.

Underwhelmed, overwhelmed,

Tinkled, and blessed;

Curiously bothered,

But no longer stressed.

A rebirth of mind, the clatter exciting;

Ideas exploding, the prospect inviting.

A daredevil dive into the abyss,

A life left behind I no longer miss.

With clarity and vision I race to the end,

A sumptuous feast around every bend.

Feeding my soul with gratitude and love,

What else could it be but the Lord up above!

It's Not Your Fault

Look at you, oh innocent child,

A guilty woman, running wild.

What goes on inside your head?

The silent words you never said.

The sins of the father, deep down inside,

Rules laid down, you honour, you abide.

The captive heart no longer free;

Manacles, chains, a prisoner,

But no one can see.

Into this world you were born,

With an innocent heart now torched and torn.

Take my hand and please don't bolt;

Always remember:

It's not your fault.

First Breath

An intake of breath,

I'm so overcome;

In less than a second,

I'll be a mum.

Green eyes watch over, etching a miracle;

Lost in a time where silence is lyrical.

As you open your eyes,

Hearts slide in the chest.

A swaddling babe, held close to my breast;

Carving your name

Won't be a dilemma.

A gift from above,

I'll call you

My Gemma.

Maud

The blooms withered and wept,

As you walked through the gate.

The birds all did cry,

As I whispered too late,

"Please don't go."

The sun lost its shine,

As you lifted the latch.

The wind did just sigh,

When you didn't quite catch,

"I'm sorry."

The tooting of horns,

The final knell,

As silence spreads,

And veils fell.

Goodbye, my friend.

Mother's Recipe

A pinch of snowy mountains,

the kind that reach the stars.

Seen from your own lenses,

not pictures on the jars.

Essence of the butterfly,

so beautifully undressed.

Then add a dash of violet,

the colour of the blessed.

Stir it very gently,

with the liquid of kind eyes,

the sort that reach

into souls,

illuminating skies.

Bind it all together,

with tender loving hands.

Share it with your neighbours,

from all the ancient lands.

With eyes that find the sidewalk,

Before they find the sky,

With tears of acid running down,

The people walk on by.

A hunched and lonely figure,

Always shrouded by a cloud,

With cardboard owned not mortgaged,

Hidden from the crowd.

With skin as hard as leather,

From the gruelling winter's bite,

Washed again in pools of shame,

But no one sees your plight.

As silence drowns out sorrow,

And pains of hunger cease,

No comfort in your bones,

The people call the police.

With no fortune in the bag,

And a life that has no feeling,

You walk along a lonely path;

It's the people who need healing.

69

When I was born in 69

all love was free

what's yours was mine

Health and safety

washing your face

knowing your neighbours

and always say

grace

CHAPTER 2

Swimming in Tears

It's the end of my first day writing poetry. Now, around four in the morning, I still write. I try to sleep, but these words won't stop. Am I going mad? Am I having a breakdown?

As I read what I have written, it becomes an evaluation of my very existence. I cry for myself and all I have been through in my life. Like a dam that has burst, I pour out my soul on paper.

I'm Swimming in Tears

I'm swimming in tears

too deep to define;

The cords lay in fragments,

the bonds lost in time.

Ice cold like winter,

my heart in a cage;

The power of thunder

lies silent in rage.

Thrashing through caverns,

wounding the skin;

Out of the dark

every sin.

Time like elastic,

bound at both ends,

unseen by those,

my saviours

and

friends.

The Fear Inside

You asked me why I run and hide,

It's nothing but the fear inside.

The reason why I cannot sleep,

Is the fear that's crouching at my feet.

The confidence I failed to find,

Is when fear crept around my mind.

I'll never find the Promised Land,

Holding fear inside my hand.

I set it free, don't build a dome;

I'll never give my fear a home.

Unique Expression

Give me the bag from off your shoulders;

let's kick away the rocks and boulders.

I'll make you laugh,

then see you smile,

as we walk up the golden mile.

Don't try to talk,

or even blink;

my arms are stronger than you think.

See the silvers, forget the blues;

there are other colours you can use.

Don't worry when the bad days come;

the clouds will fade, and show the sun.

It's only your unique expression;

for others, it is called *depression*.

Behind the Shutters

Lower the shutters – you are safe, you are well –

prepare to erase your own living hell.

The voyage began with shutters ajar,

sorting through images setting the bar.

And so it became that the flames did ignite,

pushing the buttons of fight or flight.

An infinity of exposure, of this I can tell,

will lead you to heaven,

or show you a hell.

And deep you must delve, be buoyant and brave,

honest and forthright,

find light in the cave.

Your hopes and your dreams, your heartfelt desires,

caught up in the tangles of infinite wires.

No rushing or plunder will locate the start,

a life that began with the beat of a heart.

The grain of sand hidden in valleys and glen,

take yourself back to where you were then.

Search for the smile,

the song, or a face;

hold on to it tight, then hasten the pace.

It may take some time, it may not relate,

how garbage expanded and nailed down your fate.

As the tangles unravel, unleashing the knots,

keep hold of what's needed, discard all that rots.

As the shutters re-open,

treat time like no other,

repetition bore skill,

your personal mother.

Inside Me

The road that I have travelled

bore the scars upon my feet;

The words that I have spoken

bore the smile which you greet.

The visions that stay with me

bore the love inside my breast.

The taste of giving freely

bore the thing I love the best.

The Invisible Guide

You are the glove, I am the hand;

Your vast expanse like desert sand.

A thousand thoughts you try to train,

As I run naked in the rain.

It's so immense; how do I cope?

That's when you gave me faith and hope.

The curve is random, the road so long;

My ears are open, I hear your song.

Whispering softly in the still of the night,

Open your heart, spread your wings, and take flight.

Am I the only creature to show the white of eye?

Am I the only creature to know there's more than sky?

Am I the only creature that stops to make a choice?

Am I the only creature that causes hurt with voice?

Am I the only creature who evolved to cause destruction?

Am I the only creature who cheated reproduction?

Am I the only creature to taste the sweet surrender?

Am I the only creature to hold a heart so tender?

The Sound of One Hand Clapping

When the neurons explode

as they birth a new impression,

The footsteps of your life

are your personal expression.

Keep your eyes wide open

and don't do too much napping,

and with a bit of luck,

you'll hear the sound of one hand clapping.

Mum ...

Can you hear me, Mum?

I've been calling out your name.

I've spoken to my sister,

it's great but not the same.

I know you're all around me,

I wish that I could see.

A month is such a long time,

without you calling me.

"You better ring your sister,"

that is what you'd say,

"and please always remember

she lost me too that day."

CHAPTER 3

The Prayer

It's official: I have lost my marbles. Day 2 of poetry writing, and the dam is officially wide open. The poems are coming thick and fast.

My sense of humour begins to surface, giving me some light relief. They do say that laughter is the best medicine. …

The Prayer

Oh shiver me timbers,

I feel a wreck.

I made a big blunder,

I'm up to my neck.

I ran off with Molly,

a maid from kitchen.

I'm worrying now;

you see, I've been itchin'.

My old man looks tired,

It's not a good feelin';

I'm not sure a potion will hasten the healin'.

I'll wrap it in clover and bind it with cloth,

I'll pray to the gods the thing don't drop off.

Dear Barry

I am really, really sorry,

but I had to write this letter.

We've been having problems,

and it isn't getting better.

I know you fancy Doris;

you've been flirting at the fence.

I watched you look into to her eyes;

it really was intense.

The magazine you think you hide,

well, I found it just last week.

I must admit I was surprised;

I had you down as meek.

This is really hard,

but I feel I must confess.

I'll try to do it gently,

without causing you distress.

Well, you know that I like music;

I have lessons once a week.

Besides the plucking of my strings.

there are other things that tweak.

Cymbals are my favourite,

I really like the clashing.

But later on before I leave,

there are other things I'm bashing.

There's not much more to say,

it's all so very hard.

Location of belongings

are enclosed within this card.

From,

June

X

Fine Dining

Eyes peeping out from under a visor,

A long time ago, I was younger, not wiser.

Dressed all in leather, he said he was Joe;

I can barely remember, it was so long ago.

We most definitely dined on fried fish and chips,

I remember that clearly, I tasted his lips.

That was the moment I let out a squeal;

He was no longer eating,

but having a feel!

Don't get me wrong, I wasn't whining;

after all, my old friend,

I call that fine dining!

Wonderful memories, wonderful feel;

I really enjoyed my spectacular meal.

All I Know

Look behind the wisps of hair,

the quirky old-man stoop.

Old Tom has lots to offer,

He's really quite a scoop.

His wisdom knows no boundaries,

His knowledge is pure gold.

An adequate companion,

For long nights in the cold.

He likes the heat of Zumba,

His passion lies with playing tennis.

I hope this helps,

That's all I know.

Regards from Tom's mate, Dennis

The Unmentionable Word

A perilous endeavour of which I must speak;

A dangerous journey, it's not for the weak.

I wonder if I should refrain from the issue;

Deprivation and loss, you may need a tissue.

I'll begin with you, butter, so creamy to taste;

You love me so much, you stuck to my waist.

I moan with delight at you, chocolate bar;

You expanded my hips, you just went too far.

And sugar sugar sugar, I had to say it thrice;

Rotting my teeth, they no longer look nice.

Oh juicy pork pie, although you're delicious;

I have to face facts, you're just not nutritious.

I won't say *that* word, this time I'll just do it;

I said it before, and then I just blew it.

So it's pie in the sky, and no sugar rush;

Here I go now … with a mouthful of bush.

Mmm. …

CHAPTER 4

Entwine with Me

I can't explain what happened next, apart from the fact I am single, and have been for four years. Freud would probably diagnose it as sexual frustrations.

It was in the wee hours of the morning that I wrote the poems on the pages that follow. Unable to share them with any local friends at such early hours, I rang Australia. As the director of nursing for a large Australian hospital (who happens to be my aunty) got ready for work, I shared my dirty poems with her.

Entwine with Me

Legs entwined like vines

creating a commotion.

Branches wide in girth

running deeper than an ocean.

Caverns that lay open

a welcome invitation.

Guarantee fidelity

and wondrous admiration.

The petals show their colour

a flaming crimson red.

Burning down the forest

till he lies upon her bed.

The Lie

It's hard to explain

the way that I'm feeling.

To you, I'm in charge;

Inside I am reeling.

A beautiful creature,

Before me you stand.

Your fate near to sight

With the touch of my hand.

For I cannot show you

My vulnerable side.

As I tighten the chains,

Only I know I lied.

A Proper Gent

Oh ye, pray tell, you dirty beast,

Upon my breast you come to feast?

And you a rich an proper gent,

Did you sniff my dirty scent?

Come hear the bells as they toll nine,

Now bugger off, you dirty swine.

Oh Lordy

Oh Lord, don't stop, I'm halfway there;

The glistening of soft damp hair.

Oh Lord, don't stop, it won't be right;

Don't give up on me tonight.

Oh Lord, don't stop, I'm all aquiver;

I think you reached the ancient river.

Oh Lord, don't stop, as pleasures rise;

My aching mounds are touching skies.

Oh Lord don't stop, please make it last;

You dirty rat, you came too fast.

Safe Words

Before we take the journey,

On our imaginary ship,

Let's cook up a few safe words,

In case we think it's shit.

Oh, pig, wow, fuck,

Don't tug, that's muck.

A few that I can find,

Oh holy cow, don't pull that now,

I think I've changed my mind.

Final Release

The logs are set down

As we light the fire;

A smouldering mass

Of burning desire.

The throb of the light

As I gaze at the wood;

Touches me hard

Like only it could.

Hot white like diamonds

The blistering heat;

Unable to stand

And swept off my feet.

Hands that are wandering

With fever and pitch;

Pushing the button,

Flicking the switch;

Time has no place,

The tension a mountain;

The final release,

The rush of a fountain.

Heavenly Power

When shadows awaken me deep in the night,

the beat of your heart

igniting delight.

As your amour arouses the sweet golden flower,

our bodies embrace

the heavenly power.

Silk Ropes

Silken ropes eagerly laid out,

touching silence.

Slowly your eyes lift,

they want my compliance.

As the rope binds me,

the energies shift.

The glint in your eye,

so silent so swift.

A feverish mouth

finds peace in the hide,

As rope binds together

and mends the divide.

A couple united

and bonded through lust,

Wrapped up in a blanket

of love and of trust.

The Valley

Across valleys so wide, I hear your demand,

Fair maiden so rare, I'm at your command.

A captured mind, a vision of beauty,

Green eyes that beckon me there to your duty.

Golden tresses, a treasure I can only but take,

But it's all in my dreams not while I'm awake.

The faint smell of passion about to implode,

I'm next to you now as the valleys erode.

I touch your soft skin then inhale your taste,

Curling strong hands around a small waist.

No time exists, as I explore my plunder,

Inside my girth the roaring of thunder.

As ecstasy heightens in valleys so deep,

in anticipation of what we will reap.

A rush of excitement as your body breaks,

A trembling giant whose heart is awake.

Mating Season

The savage beast,

He broke the gate.

The intense will

to procreate.

Wearing feathers,

Painted chest,

Finds his feet,

Outruns the rest.

The mating season has begun:

Take your aim,

Unload your gun.

Lollipop

Can I suck your lollipop?

I hear it tastes quite fruity.

I know I have no teeth right now, but inside I'm such a beauty.

Can I suck your lollipop?

It's shrinking by the minute.

I know I have a hairy face, but my heart will still be in it.

Can I suck your lollipop?

The colours looks amazing.

Just close your eyes and don't despise; I'm very good at grazing.

Three Minutes Later

You started out at twelve.

It's now three minutes later,

and here I stand,

hand on hip,

Holding a cheese grater.

I agree, these things can happen,

and I don't want to nag,

but you really should get sorted,

We could have decent shag!

You said that I'm too sexy; I think you're talking trash.

I know that it's been ages since we had a good old bash.

So come on, man, do something!

Three minutes is too short.

I'm open to suggestions or another kinky thought.

So glad we had this chat, I don't just think of me.

And while you mull it over, I'll have sausage for my tea.

The Criers

Stolen moments bathed in guilt, a tapestry of woven silk.

It makes doves cry, and flowers crumble, they must take care

of words that tumble.

Although they yearn to tell a nation, they must hide the dark elation.

For clothes that tear the world apart, and meetings that could break

a heart,

Will have no place inside a home, where love grows pure not under

stone.

There in the mist of weak desire, lies the whisper of the crier.

CHAPTER 5

The Shame

As I enter the third day of rhyme thought, I begin to wonder when it will end.

It's Easter weekend. I have not gotten dressed for two days. Yesterday felt quite funny, but today is sombre. I can only describe it as a shift in consciousness: I am seeing the world through a new set of lenses.

The Shame

When I forgot about the stars,

I lost my navigation.

When the sun was not my centre,

I gave away creation.

As I cut down mighty oaks,

I took more than I could use.

When the birds all disappeared,

my mind became confused.

As I walked this crooked road,

my balance started to wane.

And the stars do bathe my soul,

as I hold my head in shame.

The Story of My Shoe

The buyer's smile grows bigger,

her heart does not expand;

a mind that never wonders

of the shoes held in her hand.

The maker glues the leather

pursued by searing heat;

the stitch is always perfect,

or she won't get to eat.

The giver caged in darkness,

no fields for her to roam;

her skin the precious leather,

her voice a silent moan.

The Trouble with the Bubble

Sat inside the bubble, watching from afar;

The cuts are getting deeper,

More than just a scar.

Safe inside the bubble,

It's not affecting me;

With dead fish on the shores,

And no sign of the bee.

The trouble with the bubble is,

What happens when it bursts?

When water is pure gold,

And only kings

can quench their thirst.

The Flock

A cosmic collision that paved the way

When darkness clears my flocks astray.

Chatter of venom, the shunning of peace;

Brother fights brother, and loyalties cease.

Carving great voids in landscapes and hills;

Polluting clear waters and swallowing pills.

Slain where they stand the greatest of beasts;

Laid out on tables, the spectacular feasts.

Stumbling blindly, their path almost lost;

Innocent children who shall pay the cost.

The battles proceed to a deafening roar;

Young lives are wasted, the casualties soar.

I know the next age as I gaze from the skies;

My heart fills with love as they open their eyes.

Vibrant, full of colour, packed with awe and wonder;

Now you lay bare, the colour dimmed through plunder.

Oh, what have you done?

Said the Lord drowned in sorrow.

Where will I start to build your tomorrow?

Do I give you my breath, the job of the trees?

Oh, what did you do to the wondrous seas?

Where is the love? It flowed through your soul;

And what is this hate that plugged up the hole?

You are my children, such beautiful creatures;

Your ears blocked with sand when I sent you my teachers.

Your mother is crying, she's heaving and sobbing;

You stand on her body, the one you've been robbing.

Open your minds and feel the light stream;

And into your hearts my love I will beam. …

Amen

The Helter-Skelter

The holy man, his breath pure grace;
The other man, he hid his face.
Both stood before the hordes of men
gathered on the final glen.

The holy man, with eyes of love,
gentle like the holy dove,
could only give what is within;
there was no writing on his skin.

The other man, he held a sign
covered in a golden twine.
Water, food, warmth, and shelter;
welcome to the helter-skelter.

For those who chose to close their eyes,
wrapped up warm in webs of lies;
they slid on down into the abyss,
welcomed with a Judas kiss.

The holy man held on to hands,

as waters poured from all the lands;

the tears of every man now seen,

of what is now and what has been.

Told before in words of Scripture,

man could see the final picture;

and all that held the holy hand,

were taken to the Promised Land.

The Spirit of the One

You are the breath in Africa,

The ice upon the poles;

Not to be divided,

A singular, a whole.

You light up stars so brightly,

With your energies called love;

All knowing that to darken minds,

Restricts what thrives above.

Your tale of old gave knowledge,

Of all that is the now;

With words that know a meaning,

A math to show us how.

And time and time roam freely,

As given by your blessing;

the code entwined so deep inside,

Understandings need no guessing.

CHAPTER 6

The Seven Billion

Three days had passed, in a haze. I had written seventy poems, with no planning, no thought – it just happened.

I had been on a journey of self-discovery, and I felt a deep connection with the earth, nature, and all creatures.

I believed, and still do, that my mum sat next to me in spirit as I wrote every word. I also had a gut feeling that some of the poems I wrote were messages to me from my mum, warnings about greed and selfishness. Reminders of who I am, and that I come from love.

The Seven Billion

Seven billion stories, all of them unique,

Seven billion insights offering critique;

Seven billion voices, each sound a different vibe;

Seven billion miracles that grew from the small tribe.

Envy

Flashes of envy,

the eyes start to narrow;

here comes the pain,

a heart-piercing arrow.

A thief in the night,

no warning of entry;

eons of dark

cloak the light of my sentry.

Buried deep down,

in bottomless wrath;

disguised in the smile,

hidden in the laugh.

No intention exempt,

from the loss of the will;

the blackest of deeds,

a natural skill.

For all that is hallowed,

and all that is right,

are present no more

in the darkest of night.

The Box

Pandora's box had lost its crux,

and minds were open wide;

The secrets once held so dear,

laid out for all mankind.

The fear and lack of self-control

were useless and not needed;

And deep inside you cannot find

the word the box had heeded.

Narrow Man

All I could see was pink;
He told me it was blue.
He told me not to worry,
and accept that all is true.

All I hear is sound
vibrating on the ink;
He told me it was still,
He told me not to think.

All I taste is flavour,
where everything is sweet;
He gave me all that's bitter,
He told me I must eat.

All I touch is air
as it moves around my soul;
He tells me this is worthless,
He fills my hands with gold.

Disappearing

When all who had opinions

placed them safely on the shelf,

afraid of what would come

from revealing the true self.

As voices screamed out louder,

it really did not matter,

to debate whilst standing alone,

causing confidence to shatter.

And so it came to be

in the time that was to come,

the people swallowed tablets

to stop them feeling glum.

And it was soon forgotten

of how it used to be;

erased from every book

what was I

and what was me.

The Conductor

I can almost taste the venom,

as my ink spills on the paper;

despair in spite of courage,

as lover becomes hater.

The conductor stands unnoticed,

despite his orchestration;

the gentle movement of his hand,

creating devastation.

The vibrations of his sound,

no longer angels calling;

his piece is never finished,

until he sees the brawling.

And the song that he is singing

is darker than my fear;

oh how my body shudders

whenever he is near.

Old Speak

As the words became the power,

silent tone

and no inflection,

which left the population

to add their own injection;

with minds that flowed with worry,

spilling out from every cell,

held inside their hands,

lacking taste

and lacking smell.

And so the words hung down,

like grapes upon the vine,

rotting and fermenting

in what would be new time;

and soon they all forgot

how to address the masses,

lost within a text,

fuelled with deadly gases.

Gathering Faces

Follow all into new time,

Accentuating future crime;

Controlling what you think you like,

Expanding greed and breeding plight.

Beware when gathering in masses,

Orthodox, remove your glasses;

Omniscience is not for sale,

Knotted in this future tale.

Small Print

I explain my dilemma,
calm, clear, and with hope.

"It's in the small print,"
says the calm lady.
"I can't help you."

"Please," I retort.
My voice rising higher.
I just don't understand
Why she's fanning my fire

"It's in the small print,"
says the calm lady.
"I can't help you."

"It's unjust and unfair!"
I'm losing control.
Can she feel my despair,
and still play her role?

"It's in the small print,"
says the calm lady.
"I can't help you."

"Are you human?"
I ask, my breath
out of fight.
How can I convey
that it doesn't seem right?

"It's in the small print,"
says the calm lady.
"I can't help you."

As silence ensues,
I echo "hello."
I forgot I can't shout;
it's in the small print,
you know!

Brown Eyes

The brown eyes melt the ice of hearts

in corners of the earth;

Five years old, you pay the price

for standing on wrong turf.

Innocent and pure of heart,

caught up in worlds of power;

praying they can see you

from high up in the tower.

I hold your hand inside my mind

and hope it eases pain;

as butterflies fall to the ground,

a vision of new reign.

An Orwellian State?

I'm hearing some whispers,
"It's an Orwellian state."
So I'll take a quick look,
and join the debate.
I confirm I am worried,
It doesn't look bright.
Lots of talk
but no action,
increasing the plight.

Look back at our history,
the problem's the same;
when fighting does nothing
but increase the pain.

So what is the answer?
I'll do a quick sum:
Respect every human?
Then put down your gun.

Brave Souls

By delving in the past you'll find

the spirit that was voice of mind.

Words like *just imagine* …

or visions of a dream;

perhaps it's time to listen,

and ponder what they mean.

For they are not the last;

I'm sure that you will find

the bravest souls

that dare to share

the voice inside

their minds.

Upon the bough there sat a bird,

his song rang out to all that heard;

free to speak, a given right,

no one to judge "it's wrong, it's right";

his nest a home, not bought but free,

provided by his friend the tree;

he dined in any land he pleased,

supported by the gentle breeze;

and all this cost him not one dollar,

and he was neither rich

nor scholar;

I wonder is there room for one as I,

a taste of freedom in the sky.

Born Unfree

Born into a lie,

I was told that I was free;

If I had known the truth,

I would say,

"Please don't make me."

This godly note of paper,

Worshipped above the rest;

Without it food or shelter

will be a lifelong test.

Yet I will play my part,

and see this story through;

but if you say "you're free,"

I will say

"That's just not true."

Yesterday

If I went to sleep

and woke up yesterday,

then I would believe

the words the papers say;

I would just agree,

of course We Need To Fight!

I would be so happy that David saw the plight.

Alas, my eyes have opened

to a world that feels unjust;

sorting through opinions

of who and what I trust.

The question in my mind,

who's leading down the path?

I know we come from peace,

but all I see is wrath.

Free Pill

I went to the doctor, I've been feeling quite blue;

Headaches and panic, to name but a few.

He got out his book, and checked for a pill;

But he could not cure what was making me ill.

Through tears of pure anguish, I looked at the clock;

Three minutes of time, that was all that I got.

As I enter my home, it's dark and smells damp;

I wish I had money, I'd light up a lamp.

I swallow the water, I bought at the till;

But there must be a God, as I got a free pill.

Dalliance

The lingering glance that wrenched my peaceful heart,

a temperate touch, as lips and arms part

This union.....

oh how it makes my heart billow,

as morning breaks I wake

and I have blood on my pillow

crimson waterfalls

that flow from eyes....

as I wonder where my true loves lies.

Taxing My Feet

Delivered on time, I'll look if I dare;

I hope it's not big, my bill for fresh air.

I'm paying tomorrow, to look at the sun;

It's my special treat, so I don't feel glum.

The tax on the moon's not risen for years;

but the tax on my feet is causing some fears.

I don't say a lot, since the fee for my talk;

I hear it saves money if you learn how to squawk.

Laughter is free, but not for that long;

It's now classified as a payable song.

I had an idea, I'll give it go, the word that got banned –

I think I'll say

No!

A Tale of Two Words

The noble truths that lift man's heart eternal,

A vivid blaze that thaws the bitter night,

Like tears that flow freely, in joyous rapture,

Swathed in crimson blood never broken,

Oh invisible word, they named you Love.

Entwined in battle for eternity,

In darkened shadows your attachment lies,

An abhorrent force of the darkest day,

Foundations buried in scriptures of ancestors,

In frequent disguises they called you Hate.

They embrace akin, since earth's early dawn.

Lightning Source UK Ltd.
Milton Keynes UK
UKOW04n1448180115

244670UK00001B/12/P